CELEB

OLYMPIC STARS

LAURA DURMAN

W
FRANKLIN WATTS

First published in 2011 by
Franklin Watts
338 Euston Road
London NW1 3BH

Franklin Watts Australia
Level 17/207 Kent Street
Sydney NSW 2000

ISBN: 978 1 4451 0535 2

Dewey classification number: 796.4'8'0922

A CIP catalogue record for this book is available from the British Library.

Planning and production by Discovery Books Limited
Editor: Laura Durman
Designer: D.R. ink

Printed in China

Franklin Watts is a division of Hachette Children's Books, an Hachette UK company.
www.hachette.co.uk

Photo acknowledgements: Getty Images: pp. 3 and 27 (Popperfoto), 6 (Michael Steele),
7 (Pierre-Philippe Marcou/AFP), 8 (Jamie Squire), 9 (Andrew Yates/AFP), 10 (Mark Koble),
11 (Greg Wood/AFP), 12 (Carl De Souza/AFP), 13 (Damien Meyer/AFP), 14–15 (Michael
Kappeler/AFP), 16–17 (Harry How), 17 (AFP), 18–19 (Alexander Hassenstein/Bongarts),
19 (Fabrice Coffrini/AFP), 20–21 (Philippe Lopez/AFP), 21 and 29 (AFP), 23 (AFP), 24 (Liu
Jin/AFP), 26 (Pascal Rondeau); Rex Features: p. 25 (Photoshot Holdings Ltd.); Shutterstock
Images: pp. 5 (Robert Adrian Hillman), 22 (Lev Radin); Wikimedia: pp. 15 (Brunel University).

Cover photos: Getty Images: Jessica Ennis (Ian Walton/Aviva), Usain Bolt (Gabriel Bouys/
AFP), Sir Chris Hoy (Carl De Souza/AFP).

Note to parents and teachers:
Every effort has been made by
the Publishers to ensure that the
websites in this book are suitable
for children, that they are of the
highest educational value, and
that they contain no inappropriate
or offensive material. However,
because of the nature of the
Internet, it is impossible to
guarantee that the contents of
these sites will not be altered.
We strongly advise that Internet
access is supervised by a
responsible adult.

CONTENTS

Words in **bold** are in the glossary.

JESSICA ENNIS

Jessica Ennis is one of the world's greatest athletes. Although she has yet to compete at an Olympic Games, Team GB has high hopes that Jessica will win gold in the **heptathlon** at the 2012 Olympics.

Ennis competes in the high jump at the World Indoor Championships in Doha, Qatar.

EARLY DAYS

Ennis joined her local athletics club at the age of 11. She began competing in junior and youth competitions at the age of 14 and showed great promise as a **multi-eventer**. In her breakthrough year, 2005, she won gold in the heptathlon at the European Athletics Junior Championships and bronze at the World University Games in Izmir, Turkey.

SENIOR ATHLETICS

In her first **senior** season, Ennis took bronze in the heptathlon at the Commonwealth Games in Melbourne in March 2006. At the 2007 **IAAF** World Combined Events Challenge in Italy, Ennis equalled the British high jump record of 1.95m. Later that year at the World Championships in Osaka, Japan, Ennis finished fourth in the heptathlon. Although she narrowly missed out on a medal, she did achieve a **personal best** points total of 6,469.

FROM DISASTER TO SUCCESS

Although Ennis qualified for the 2008 Olympic Games in Beijing, she was forced to pull out due to a **stress fracture** in her ankle. She mounted an impressive comeback in 2009, winning the 2009 IAAF Combined Events Challenge in Italy and entered the World Championships as favourite to win. Ennis did not disappoint. She led from the very first event and came out on top, winning the gold medal with a personal best of 6,731 points. In 2010, she became the World Indoor **Pentathlon** Champion and won the heptathlon at the European Championships that year, too.

CELEB BIO

Date of birth	**28 January 1986**
Place of birth	**Sheffield, England**
Height	**1.65m**
Greatest achievement	**Becoming 2010 World Heptathlon Champion**

'Though I do think about 2012, I try not to worry about it – it's something that I want to enjoy and make the most of, not something I'm dreading.'

FACT

Ennis set a new championship record at the World Indoor Pentathlon Championship in 2010 when she took gold with 4,937 points. She then repeated this feat at the European Athletic Championships, winning heptathlon gold with 6,823 points – a new personal best and new championship record.

SIR CHRIS HOY

FACT
Hoy spends up to 35 hours a week training in the gym, on the road and at the cycle track.

adidas

GREAT BRITAIN
BEIJING 2008

adidas

Hoy celebrates as he takes the gold medal in the sprint event at the 2008 Beijing Olympic Games.

CELEB BIO

Date of birth	**23 March 1976**
Place of birth	**Edinburgh, Scotland**
Height	**1.86m**
Greatest achievement	**Winning three gold medals at the 2008 Beijing Olympics**

Hoy sprints past on the outside of his opponent to become 2008 World Sprint Champion.

Track cycling is a fast and furious Olympic sport that requires endurance, power, speed and tactics. Sir Chris Hoy is the most successful Olympic male track cyclist of all time.

ALL-ROUNDER

During his school years Chris played team sports, proving himself to be a great all-round sportsman. However, he later discovered that he preferred competing on his own rather than relying on a team. **BMX** gave him the freedom that he craved and, by the age of 14, he had become Scottish Champion, ranked second in Britain and ninth in the world.

ONTO THE TRACK

At the age of 16, Hoy turned his attention to track sprint cycling. At his very first race he stated his goal of becoming a champion in the 2004 Olympic Games. Although most people laughed at the time, Hoy did go on to win his first Olympic gold in 2004 in the **kilo** event. For the 2008 Olympic Games,

Hoy focused on three different track cycling events – the **sprint**, **team sprint** and **keirin**. He became the first Briton since 1908 to win three Olympic gold medals at the same Games. In 2009 Hoy was awarded a **knighthood** for his achievements.

INTENSITY

Hoy claims that intensity is the key to his success. He puts in 100 per cent effort to every training session to ensure that, by race time, he has done everything possible to prepare himself. He also has an incredible ability to focus during a race, blocking out everything from the crowd to TV cameras. He allows instinct to take over, which is vital in a sport where a split-second decision can make the difference between winning or losing. All of this gives Hoy every chance of repeating his successes at the 2012 Games.

'Once the race is on… it's man on man, it's just about being the first to cross the line.'

'Now I've just got one more title to get before the end of my career and that is the Olympic gold. So that's the aim.'

TOM DALEY

Diving is an adrenaline-fuelled competitive sport that reaches dizzying heights – literally! By the age of 15 Tom Daley had already become a British Champion, European Champion, World Champion and competed in an Olympic Games.

Daley proudly shows the gold medal that he won in the Men's 10m Platform Final at the 2010 Commonwealth Games in Delhi.

YOUNG TALENT

Daly is the youngest ever British World Champion in any sport. He began diving at the age of seven and quickly showed natural **flair** and talent. Incredibly Daly has never been beaten in his age group at any National Championship event. Although he did not win any medals at the 2008 Olympics, onlookers were still impressed by this young man's drive, **poise** and performance. In 2010 he won two gold medals at the Commonwealth Games in Delhi, India. Team GB has high hopes for this young sportsman at the 2012 London Olympics.

AN OPINIONATED SPORT

At diving competitions seven judges score each dive. The marks awarded are solely based on each judge's opinion. A perfect dive is when all seven judges award you ten marks for the dive. Daley has performed two perfect dives in his career – one in a synchronised event with partner Blake Aldridge, and one in the individual event at the 2010 Commonwealth Games.

CELEBRITY IN CHINA

In China, divers are treated in the same way as Premier League footballers are in the UK. Daley regularly visits China for competitions and enjoys the attention he attracts. He is even said to have had several marriage proposals from young Chinese fans! Daley is a popular figure back in the UK, too. In 2010 he was nominated for the BBC Sports Personality of the Year.

CELEB BIO

Date of birth **21 May 1994**

Place of birth **Plymouth, England**

Height **1.7m**

Greatest achievements **Winning two gold medals at the 2010 Commonwealth Games**

The judges awarded Daley maximum points at the Commonwealth Games for this dive.

BETH TWEDDLE

Gymnastics has always been an important part of the Olympic Games. Male and female gymnasts demonstrate grace, skill and strength in this popular sport. One of the leading lights is Beth Tweddle – Britain's most successful gymnast ever.

GYMNASTIC EVENTS

There are three different gymnastic disciplines at the Olympic Games – artistic, **rhythmic** and trampoline. Artistic gymnastics is the oldest discipline and is performed using different types of **apparatus**, such as the **uneven bars**, **table** and **balance beam**. Competitions are held to find the best team, the best individual on a particular apparatus and the best all-round gymnast. Tweddle's signature event is the uneven bars.

ENERGY AND FOCUS

Tweddle was an extremely energetic child, and started gymnastics at the age of seven. The coaches at her local club quickly recognised her potential. At the age of nine she became a member of the British junior national team and, five years later, became British Junior Vice-Champion. Having progressed to the senior team, she became British All-round Champion in 2001 and won gold at the 2002 Commonwealth Games. In 2006, Tweddle became Britain's very first World Champion by winning the uneven bars event.

OLYMPIC GAMES

Tweddle competed in the 2004 Olympic Games, taking part in both the team and individual competitions. Although Tweddle was hopeful of success, she finished in nineteenth position. She fared much better at the 2008 Beijing Games, qualifying for the uneven bars final. Unfortunately, she narrowly missed out on a medal, finishing fourth. She has gone on to win the 2009 and 2010 World Championships in the floor and uneven bars events and has high hopes of winning a medal at the 2012 Games.

Tweddle performs a gold medal-winning routine on the uneven bars.

CELEB BIO

Date of birth **1 April 1985**

Place of birth **Johannesburg, South Africa**

Height **1.61m**

Greatest achievements **Claiming her third World Championship gold**

Tweddle poses with her gold after winning the floor event at the 2009 World Championships.

'I've got every title to my name now apart from an Olympic one and I'd be happy with any Olympic medal, it doesn't have to be gold.'

NEED FOR SPEED

USAIN BOLT

CELEB BIO

Date of birth **21 August 1986**

Place of birth **Trelawny, Jamaica**

Height **1.95m**

Greatest achievement **Running the 100m in a world record time of 9.58 seconds**

'People always say I'm a legend, but I'm not. Not until I've defended my Olympic titles. That's when I've decided I'll be a legend.'

Track athletics remains one of the most popular sports in the Olympic Games. Usain Bolt is arguably the most naturally gifted athlete the world has ever seen.

JOURNEY TO SUCCESS

Bolt's first athletics medal was earned at school, but surprisingly it was awarded for hurdles rather than sprinting. From the age of 14 he began competing in regional and national championships in Jamaica. He took gold in the 200m race at the 2002 World Junior Championships in Kingston, the 2003 World Youth Championships in Canada, and the 2004 Carifta Games in Hamilton, Bermuda (where he broke the world junior record). His potential as a senior World Champion contender was clear to see.

OLYMPIC DEBUT

Bolt first entered the Olympic Games in 2008. He stunned the world when he became the first man in Olympic history to win both the 100m and 200m races in world record times. He then took part in the 4x100m relay team and smashed the world record once again. This incredible performance earned him the title of 'The fastest man in the world'.

OUT OF THE ORDINARY

Bolt stands out as an unusual character in the world of athletics – not only because of his talent. While his competitors focus and seriously warm up for a race, Bolt tends to look relaxed, smile and sometimes even dances for his fans! He is also surprisingly tall, standing at 1.95m. Finally he suffers from a condition called **scoliosis** which has left him with one leg shorter than the other – something that you might have expected would rule out a career in sport!

FACT

Bolt has a signature lightning-bolt pose, called the Bolt Arms, which he uses to celebrate victory.

MICHAEL PHELPS

Michael Phelps is an Olympic hero who has dominated his sport like no other. Having beaten the record for winning the most gold medals in one Olympic Games in 2008, he is one of the top Olympians of all time.

EARLY DAYS

Phelps started swimming at the age of five. Having been diagnosed with **ADHD**, he used swimming as a positive way to release his energy and began swimming competitively. By the age of ten he had his first national record. Phelps qualified for the 2000 Sydney Olympics at the age of 15, making him the youngest member of the US team since 1932. He was placed fifth in the 200m butterfly competition. The following year, he set a new record for this event at the World Championships in Fukuoka, Japan, making him the youngest swimming world record holder.

ATHENS

On the first day of the 2004 Olympic Games in Athens, Phelps won the 400m individual **medley** event and set a new world record. On the fourth day of competition, he beat Takashi Yamamoto to win the 200m butterfly and, an hour later, led the 4x200m freestyle relay team to victory. Finally he took individual gold medals in the 100m butterfly and 200m individual medley, as well as a team gold in the 4x100m medley relay. Having also won two bronze medals, Phelps' eight-medal haul established his position in the history books.

BEIJING

At the 2008 Beijing Games, Phelps set his sights on beating US swimming legend Mark Spitz's record of winning seven gold medals at one Olympic Games. He reached his target and beat it, taking eight gold medals and setting one Olympic record and an incredible seven world records! He also tied the record for the number of individual gold medals won at an Olympic Games. Phelps currently ranks second in total career Olympic medals, but hopes to change this at the 2012 Games.

Phelps powers through the water at the US National Championships in Irvine, California.

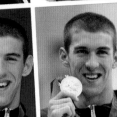

Phelps shows off the eight gold medals that he won at the 2008 Beijing Olympic Games.

CELEB BIO

Date of birth **30 June 1985**

Place of birth **Baltimore, USA**

Height **1.93m**

Greatest achievement **Winning eight gold medals at the 2008 Olympic Games**

'Records are always made to be broken no matter what they are ... Anybody can do anything that they set their mind to.'

FACT

By the age of 25, Phelps had won 50 gold medals in major international competitions.

YELENA ISINBAYEVA

Yelena Isinbayeva has been hailed as the queen of global athletics. This charismatic Russian athlete has achieved an astonishing amount since her breakthrough in 2004.

YOUNG DREAMS

Isinbayeva grew up in a tiny apartment in the former Soviet Union. She dreamed of becoming a gymnast, following in the footsteps of successful Soviets such as Nellie Kim and Olga Korbut. Her parents worked hard to support her dreams, and by the age of ten she was a national champion. However, by the time Isinbayeva was 15, her dreams were shattered when she grew too tall to be a gymnast. Fortunately, she was encouraged to take up the pole vault instead.

EARLY SUCCESS

Within less than a year of taking up pole vaulting, Isinbayeva became champion at the 1998 World Youth Games in Moscow. In 2000, the year that the women's pole vault became an Olympic event, Isinbayeva vaulted her way to victory at the World Junior Championships in Santiago, Chile. She took her first senior medal in 2002 and, the following year, set her first world record with a leap of 4.82m.

OLYMPICS

Isinbayeva won Olympic gold during her first Games in Athens, 2004. She broke a world record just after midnight in the memorable final. In 2008 she stamped out all of the competition to defend her title at the Beijing Games. Her vault of 5.05m smashed the 5m barrier and she once again set a new Olympic and world record. Isinbayeva increased the world record to 5.06m a year later.

FACT

Isinbayeva is mentored by Ukrainian pole vaulting legend Sergei Bubka. Bubka broke 35 records during his pole vaulting career and, in 2010, Isinbayeva announced that it was her goal to beat this!

'I like to be on top and break world records.'

Isinbayeva celebrates setting a new world record at the IAAF Golden League in Zurich, Switzerland.

CELEB BIO

Date of birth **3 June 1982**

Place of birth **Volgograd, Russia**

Height **1.74m**

Greatest achievements **Winning gold medals at the 2004 and 2008 Olympic Games**

Isinbayeva jumps in the women's pole vault final during the 2009 IAAF World Athletics Championships.

www.yelenaisinbaeva.com/en/

LIU XIANG

'(The 2012 Olympics) will give me another chance to show people what I can do. I hope I will be able to take advantage of this opportunity.'

CELEB BIO

Date of birth **13 July 1983**

Place of birth **Shanghai, China**

Height **1.89m**

Greatest achievement **Winning a gold medal in the 2004 Olympics**

Xiang hurdles his way to second place at the Golden Grand Prix in Shanghai.

Olympic hurdlers need the speed of a sprinter and extreme precision to enable them to glide over the hurdles that stand between them and the finish line. One of the most determined hurdlers of recent years is Chinese hero Liu Xiang.

STARTING OUT

Liu Xiang was always destined for a career in sports, but originally trained as a high jumper. However, it was noted that he had the perfect build for a hurdler, so he decided to switch events. In May 2001, Xiang took gold in the 110m hurdles at the East Asian Games in Japan. Later that year he made his mark on the world stage by winning at the World University Games in Beijing. In May 2004, Xiang achieved a personal dream when he beat his hero, and four-time world champion, Allen Johnson from the USA.

THE 2004 GAMES

Xiang was an obvious choice for the Chinese Olympic athletics team. He claimed China's very first gold medal in a track athletics event on 27 August. His winning time in the 110m hurdles final – 12.91 seconds – equalled Welsh hurdler Colin Jackson's world record, set in 1993. The whole of China celebrated and Xiang's status as a celebrity and national hero was established.

DISASTER STRIKES

China focused a lot of its attention on Liu Xiang during the build-up to the 2008 Beijing Olympics in China. Having won the 2007 World Outdoors and 2008 World Indoors Championships, the country held high hopes of him defending his Olympic title. However, disaster struck when Xiang was forced to limp off the track during the first **heat** with an injury to his right foot. Xiang's devastation was evident and the crowd was shocked into silence. However, having claimed his third Asian Games Championship title in 2010, Xiang is determined to recover and fight to regain his title at the 2012 Olympics.

Beijing pedestrians walk past a huge billboard featuring Xiang during the build-up to the 2008 Olympic Games.

RAFAEL NADAL

Rafael Nadal knows what it means to be at the top of your game. Having turned professional at the age of 15, he has risen through the ranks to become tennis World Number 1 in 2008.

TRAINING UP

Nadal began playing tennis at the age of four with his uncle, Toni Nadal, at his home in Mallorca, Spain. Toni, a former professional tennis player, recognised Nadal's talent and passion for the sport and began coaching him. In 2003 Rafael won the first professional match he played, and was awarded the **ATP** Newcomer of the Year trophy. By the age of 16, Nadal was already **ranked** in the world's top 50 players.

BATTLE FOR THE TOP SPOT

Nadal achieved the Number 2 ranking in July 2005, with only Roger Federer above him. In 2006, 2007 and 2008 Nadal played and beat Federer on the clay courts at the **French Open**, a tournament which Nadal dominated in the late 2000s. But Federer had the upper hand at the annual Wimbledon Championship, which is played on grass. That was until the peak of their rivalry in 2008 when Nadal triumphed against Federer in the longest final in Wimbledon history, beating him 9–7 in the deciding set.

GOING FOR GOLD

In August 2008, Nadal competed in the Olympic Games for the first time. He won the men's singles competition, claiming the first ever gold medal for Spain in Olympic tennis. In the same month, Nadal finally overtook Federer in the rankings, officially becoming World Number 1.

ONWARDS AND UPWARDS

In 2009 Nadal was troubled with a knee injury and Federer moved back up to Number 1. However, Nadal made a strong comeback in 2010, winning the French Open, Wimbledon and the **US Open** and reclaiming the Number 1 ranking. He is looking forward to defending his Olympic title at the 2012 Games in London on the Wimbledon courts.

Despite being fierce rivals, Federer and Nadal have a lot of respect for each other and are said to be good friends off the court.

CELEB BIO

Date of birth	3 June 1986
Place of birth	Mallorca, Spain
Height	1.85m
Greatest achievement	Achieving a career Golden Slam in 2010 (see fact box)

'The Olympic Games are the most special... Here, I won for my country – not only for me. It's a very different feeling (from a Grand Slam) – you get this chance only every four years.'

Nadal competes at the Beijing Olympics on his way to winning gold.

ELLIE SIMMONDS

CELEB BIO

Date of birth **11 November 1994**

Place of birth **Walsall, West Midlands**

Height **1.23m**

Greatest achievement **Winning two gold medals at the Beijing Paralympic Games**

Ellie Simmonds celebrates after winning and setting a new world record in the 400m freestyle final during the 2008 Beijing Paralympics.

Ellie Simmonds was a keen swimmer from a young age. After watching the Athens **Paralympic** Games in 2004 on television, she became determined to compete one day. This dream came true just four years later in Beijing.

Simmonds and her coach Billy Pye have both been awarded **MBEs** by the Queen.

THE PARALYMPIC GAMES

The first Paralympic Games was organised in Rome in 1960, and featured 400 disabled athletes from 23 different countries. Since then the Paralympic Games has grown to become an **elite** sporting event that focuses on athletic achievements, and not disability. The 2008 Games in Beijing attracted 3,951 athletes from 146 countries. Ellie Simmonds achieved her goal of taking part in the Games and, aged 13, was the youngest member of the British team.

SWIMMING START

Simmonds was born with achondroplasia, a form of **dwarfism**. That didn't stop her having a talent and enthusiasm for swimming. After watching the 2004 Paralympics, she began to train harder and more seriously. When the British Disability High Performance Centre was set up at the Wales National Pool in Swansea, Simmonds was determined to train there. She persuaded her mother to live in Swansea with her during the week so that she could follow her dream. Under the direction of head coach Billy Pye, Simmonds developed a demanding training programme that prepared her for international competition.

BEIJING BONANZA

Simmonds won two gold medals at the 2008 Paralympic Games in Beijing. She produced an astonishing surge of power in the last 25m of the 100m freestyle event, racing up from fourth position to take the lead from favourite Mirjam de Koning-Peper of the Netherlands. She also won the 400m freestyle race and competed in three further events. Simmonds is Britain's youngest ever individual Paralympic gold medallist. Having won four gold medals and broken three world records at the World Paralympic Swimming Championships in 2010, the British team has high hopes for Simmonds at the London Games in 2012.

FACT

Simmonds won the BBC Young Sports Personality of the Year award in 2008, and was the youngest person to ever receive an MBE from the Queen in 2009.

'Being small never stopped her doing anything and there was never anything she felt she couldn't do!'

VAL SIMMONDS, ELLIE'S MOTHER

SIR STEVE REDGRAVE

'(From the age of) 16 or 17, I was setting myself targets of trying to get to the Olympic Games and hopefully win!'

Steve Redgrave rows his way to victory in the 1996 Atlanta Games.

Redgrave (left) poses with his British teammates Tim Foster, James Cracknell and Matthew Pinsent (L-R) after winning the gold in the men's **coxless fours** rowing final at the Sydney Olympics.

Sir Steve Redgrave is a British sporting icon and an Olympic legend. He is one of only four Olympians ever to win gold medals at five consecutive Olympic Games.

THE OLYMPICS

Redgrave first struck gold at the 1984 Olympic Games in Los Angeles in the coxless fours event. He then joined up with Andy Holmes to win gold in the **coxless pairs** at the next Olympic Games, held in Seoul, South Korea. Redgrave continued with the event, but teamed up with Matthew Pinsent to win at the 1992 Barcelona Games and the 1996 Olympics in Atlanta. James Cracknell and Tim Foster joined the pair to compete in the coxless fours in 2000, winning Redgrave's historic fifth gold medal.

OTHER ACHIEVEMENTS

Although Redgrave is best-known for his Olympic medals, he has achieved many other things during his career. He has claimed nine World Championships and won the Silver Goblets & Nickalls' Challenge Cup at the Henley Royal Regatta a record seven times. He became a triple Commonwealth medallist in 1986. In 2001 he was awarded a knighthood in recognition of his sporting achievements.

LIFE AFTER ROWING

Since retiring, Redgrave has used his celebrity to forge a career outside sport. He often provides an expert opinion on television coverage of rowing events. He has also featured in high-profile TV adverts for companies such as Flora ProActiv and Ultralase. At the age of 35 Redgrave was diagnosed with the medical condition **diabetes**. However, he did not let this stop him from achieving sporting success. Today he helps to raise funds and awareness of the disease. He also does a lot of other work for charity, setting up The Sir Steve Redgrave Charitable Trust in 2001. The Trust joined forces with Sport Relief in 2008 and became The Steve Redgrave Fund. The charity aims to use the power of sport to improve young people's lives.

CELEB BIO

Date of birth	**23 March 1962**
Place of birth	**Marlow, England**
Height	**1.86m**
Greatest achievement	**Winning five gold medals at five different Olympic Games**

GLOSSARY

ADHD Attention deficit hyperactivity disorder. This includes a range of behavioural disorders that include symptoms such as hyperactivity and poor concentration.

apparatus The equipment that gymnasts perform on.

ATP The Association of Tennis Professionals, who organise the men's worldwide tennis tour.

balance beam A narrow wooden beam upon which female gymnasts balance while performing exercises in competitions.

BMX A bicycle designed to be ridden on a dirt track.

coxless fours A rowing event in which a team of four competes.

coxless pairs A rowing event in which a team of two competes.

diabetes An illness in which a person has too much sugar in their blood.

dwarfism The medical term for someone who is unusually small.

elite Of the highest standard.

endurance The ability of an athlete to exert his- or herself for a long period of time.

flair The ability to do something very well.

French Open A major tennis tournament held each year in Paris.

Grand Slam tournament In tennis, one of the world's top four competitions: the French Open, Wimbledon, the US Open or the Australian Open.

heat A preliminary round in which the fastest competitors qualify for the next race.

heptathlon A combined athletics event made up of seven different events: 200 metres, 800 metres, 100 metres hurdles, high jump, long jump, shot-put and javelin.

IAAF The International Association of Athletics Federations.

keirin A 2-kilometre cycling race in which six to eight riders race behind a motorised bike for 1,400 metres. They are then released to sprint the final 600 metres.

kilo A 1,000-metre track cycling event. The kilo time trial was removed from the Olympics programme after the 2004 Games.

knighthood A special award given by the British Queen. Knights are given the title 'Sir' or 'Dame'.

MBE MBE stands for Member of the Order of the British Empire. It is awarded for services to the country or community.

medley A swimming race in which contestants swim different sections in different strokes.

mentored Advised or trained.

multi-eventer An athlete who competes in multiple events.

Paralympics An international athletics competition for athletes with disabilities.

pentathlon A contest in which athletes compete in five different events.

personal best An athlete's best ever time or score in competition.

poise Grace, elegance and composure.

professional A sportsperson who is paid for their activities.

rank Position in a table of players listed by ability.

rhythmic A discipline of gymnastics that combines gymnastics and dance. Only female athletes compete in this discipline.

scoliosis An abnormal curve of the spine.

senior A senior tournament is for older or more experienced competitors.

sprint A track cycling event in which two riders start from the same point on the track and race for three laps.

stress fracture A fracture (broken bone) that results from excessive, repetitive activity.

table A metal piece of equipment with a padded and springy cover used in the gymnastics event called the vault.

tactics Actions that have been carefully planned in order to achieve success.

team sprint A track cycling event in which two teams of three riders race to finish three laps the quickest (or catch the opposing team).

uneven bars A pair of bars of different heights used by female gymnasts in competitions. Also known as the asymmetric bars.

US Open A major tennis tournament held each year in New York, USA.

BOOKS

Olympic Sports: Athletics, by Clive Gifford (Franklin Watts, 2011)

Olympic Sports: Cycling by Clive Gifford (Franklin Watts, 2011)

Olympic Sports: Gymnastics by Clive Gifford (Franklin Watts, 2011)

Olympic Sports: Swimming and Diving by Clive Gifford (Franklin Watts, 2011)

Olympics 2012: Behind the Scenes at the Olympics (Wayland, 2011)

The Olympics: Events by Moira Butterfield (Franklin Watts, 2011)

The Olympics: Records by Moira Butterfield (Franklin Watts, 2011)

WEBSITES

www.london2012.com

The official website for the 2012 Games.

www.iaaf.org

The home of world athletics.

www.paralympics.org.uk

The official website for the British Paralympic Association (BPA).

www.olympic.org

The official website of the Olympic movement.